Reading Wind

Carol Barrett

Third Place Winner of The Poetry Box Chapbook Prize 2023

Poems © 2024 Carol Barrett, with the exception of
  "Drug Thieves at the Doctor's Office" (1991); "Pleural Effusion" (2017)
  JAMA (Journal of the American Medical Association), reprinted with
  permission granted via payment to Copyright Clearance Center, Dec 2023.
All rights reserved.

Editing & Book Design by Shawn Aveningo Sanders
Cover Image licensed via Envato
Cover Design by Shawn Aveningo Sanders
Author Photo (p.49) by Sarah Sargent

No part of this book may be republished without permission
from the author, except in the case of brief quotations
embodied in critical essays, epigraphs, reviews and articles,
or publisher/author's marketing collateral.

Third Place Winner of The Poetry Box Chapbook Prize 2023
ISBN: 978-1-956285-51-2
Published in the United States of America.
Wholesale Distribution by Ingram Group

Published by The Poetry Box®, February 2024
Portland, Oregon, United Sates
website: ThePoetryBox.com

Dedicated to the memory of my father, Dr. Marion A. Clark

A Note from the Author

These poems were inspired by my father, a rural physician, musician, and farmer. In his medical practice, he would often make the rounds of patients in their homes on a Sunday afternoon, bringing our family along for the ride. (It was not unusual to be invited in for cookies or lemonade.) My father co-founded the Southwest Washington Symphony, believing the opportunity to play there would encourage strong musicians to come teach in area high schools. He himself played baritone in the group, then took up cello because, he said, he got tired of counting rests. He was second-chair cellist into his nineties. But though he practiced as a surgeon and wielded a bow, his hands were never far from the earth. He was happy building a rock wall, grafting a branch on an apple tree, trimming his roses, or running his rototiller for the next crop of corn, beans, squash, carrots. Things came alive for him, and my hope is that his life will come alive in these poems. Whatever your experience of fathers or fathering, may these words encourage your creative pursuits, your own readings of the wind that hovers about us.

—Carol Barrett

Contents

Baby Teeth	7
Columbia	9
Blessing	10
Drug Thieves at the Doctor's Office	12
Reading Wind	14
The Bird	15
Sorting My Father's Books	17
The Tempering	19
Going Out in Style	21
The Last Sleep	22
Pleural Effusion	23
Holding the Rain	24
Going Up	28
Breathing with Boulders	29
Cutting Limbs	31
Morning Constitutional:	32
Hill Haven	34
The Order of Things	36
Messengers	39
Elegy for My Father's Passing	41
Acknowledgments	43
Early Praise	45
About the Author	49
About The Poetry Box Chapbook Prize	51

Baby Teeth
~after Kathleen Flenniken's Plume

Imagine them all laid out on silver trays,
each tiny cusp sent swift as an arrow

from Cupid, rows and rows of successive
generations, originating near Hanford

on the Columbia, moving along the wind's
impartial trajectory, farms laden

with Idaho potatoes, Montana river valleys
where trout still arch, flick rainbows in the sun.

Recall the insignia infant on every box
of Gerber Baby Cereal, that blue

shadowed lock of hair. Gerber promised
rebates for baby teeth, mailed in, perfect

pearls innocent as little bronzed shoes.
Hooded figures calculate how many

radioactive isotopes are showing up
over what range of motion, what increments

of time, and silence. In this plutonium
town, tumbleweed blows in bundles,

children dress their dolls for tea parties,
run toy trucks over the dusty backyard

grass under filmy light from the place
their fathers inhale behind locked doors,

[. . .]

decades, if they last, samples of morning
urine in milk bottles set out for collection

on front porches. Downwind in Longview
my father estimates the thickness of lead

for the basement fallout shelter where
mother has stacked rows of canned peaches,

gallon jugs of water, sleeping bags
in case the Russians drop their bomb.

But the fallout has already come.
And teeth tell: it's *American*.

Columbia

Maybe because he can trace the family back on two sides to both Meriwether Lewis and William Clark, my father yearned after the expedition trail. He bought a canoe and persuaded his new son-in law to push off down the Columbia. Packed with the first day's provisions, they paddled with the current. A few hours out they ran smack into a gale. Took every bit of brain and brawn to keep from capsizing, an old logging chain dropped in the hold for ballast, shoulders working like oxen.

The first thing that saved them was blowing into a sand dune in the middle of the fog. They crawled out, hunkered under ponchos, and waited out the torrents, canoe against their backs like a great whale bone.

Overnight they parceled cold sandwiches and stared into the face of machismo—no water, no matches, a low-lying mass without color or flares. The second saving grace was my younger brother. They couldn't risk his life with their own, stayed put till the whitecaps bobbed like mere ghosts.

My father's respect for Lewis and Clark has blown wide as the wind. But he has decided he'd rather be related to Sacajawea.

Who knows, maybe he is.

Blessing

My father recalls gooseberries rising
to the top of pies, wild Kansas fields,
stickery and hot. An earned offering.

We invent uses, this lowly plum
relic of currants: tart marmalade
oozing over goat's milk cheese,

saffron sauce, the gold coin of lamb,
fluted scallions with romaine and pear.
The prophets of Genesis reaped carob

from locust trees, ladled raw honey.
The humble gooseberry, translucent
globe lined for longitude, still

flourishes, olive gray branches
arranged in slender vases
with purple vetch. Its yield,

five hundred shekels, weeping stems
that root wherever they touch
ground, buds becoming

a quatrain of flowers. My father
planted the bristly berries
with limestone in the high shade

of persimmon, thorn at each axil,
tended through the great winter
chill when the honeybees froze,

their box of trays knocked over
by an unknown intruder, human
or beast, no matter—they were

gone when he found them
on his morning rounds.
My mother baked a steaming pie

from a quart put up at the height
of harvest, tending this loss.
She is still tending, bees

swimming the air again
as she folds her apron, rings
the big brass bell. Table filled,

cousins in from haying,
layered with sun dust. Jacob,
the youngest, leans to his plate,

licks the last sweet swirl,
a devouring without grace
but with my father's blessing.

Drug Thieves at the Doctor's Office

My father's urology practice
dealt in slow cash. In a small town
everything trickles at once.
He'd poke and prod, quiz them
like a teacher who knows
no sure thing.
They'd suit up, then follow him
to the rose patch. The options
all laid out, they'd pick the best:
First Love, Sutter's Gold, Don Juan,
High Noon, Carousel, Red Glory.
Knife in hand he'd travel the blooms,
dropping a few cabbage-heads
from the Lancaster and York,
a dark bruise from the Oakington Ruby,
then snip a single bud of Peace
or Mojave, its older cousins regaling
the colors of patient care.
If they weren't too ashamed
of slim pickings, it was theirs.
(They never were.) Even the old men
with prostates flaring would recollect
some widow down the block, sortie
simmering on the way out the door.

If cutting were the plan, he'd spell
the risk long-hand, every inch
his tools would touch deftly
mapped in a swift diagram,
pencil held at point like a thin
blade penetrating the layers
of jovial fat and striated muscle,
the intricate bones of his hands

entering the cave of their souls
like a small bird.
Stone, leak, water, flow—
he never used words they didn't know.
Common payment: a bushel
of Royal Annes, a box of early
bantam. His favorite bill:
two chinook from the wide
Columbia, their gills still going.
Complicated cases, he'd net
half a side of beef, or a full
truckload of ripe manure
for his Mt. Shasta and Golden Fleece.

The drug thieves came and went.
Their part in the annals of Cowlitz County
snuck into bloom—not the screwdrivers
that forced the lock; the only
costly equipment, a luminous microscope
still tracking the enemies
of men and rose leaves.
Missing: four syringes, seven
carefully calibrated jars
of fresh urine
from the small refrigerator
next to my mother's picture,
a glorious Queen Elizabeth
not quite unfurled.

Reading Wind

When yellow light drifts down soft as dove wings folding,
my father would say *storm coming.* He would read the wind

rustling cornstalks, plum leaves turning their silver sides out,
trying to hang on to the least limb. He always got it right,

these predictions of storm and current, gale and flash.
Raised in wanton fields of Kansas, he could feel the sky

fuming miles before the hail spun out on the road, flattened
the new crop of wheat, rattled eaves. Even the night skies

taught him, sleeping on a porch beneath a pale moon,
creek rising, twigs snapping when the dog split for cover.

He'd be right again tonight. The weather service has hailed
a record heat warning, Fahrenheit to soar the next two days,

thunder lurking in the tallest pines, wrestling with our perfect,
our unnatural plans. We never quite know when it will hit.

But when it does, my cat will peer out study window, click
her teeth as if she has spotted cougar in a prickly bush.

Then slowly back down to the comfort of an old blanket,
the air outside succumbing to the staggering dark.

The Bird
~for my mother and father

They thumb through *Birds of the Northwest*
trying to name a newcomer. I too
catch his act this morning at the suet feeder

swinging between the camellias, yellow beak
(my father is sure of it) nibbling cautiously
while tail feathers bobble. Ever since

courting they have tracked the migrations
of aerial friends. They talk eyes, and wings.
They are sure this tail has streaks of white.

See. There. Too small for a wren or sparrow,
he defies I.D. This worn slim volume
has witnessed their rarest sightings,

decade after decade whenever need
darts about. The cover is ruffled, pages
smudged, vestiges of butterhorns, perhaps

our version of suet. They settle finally
on Common Thatch, as the light
breast and black head fit the scriptural

habitat west of the Cascades. I expected
a more exotic tribute, given their whispered
wonderment, heads tilted together.

The bird, now named and known, pecks
his way into their glad world, flits
to a rafter to watch the watchers.

[. . .]

They are between surgeries, my mother
for crushed vertebrae due to a fall
on the slate beneath the feeders,

my father for cataracts splitting his pine
trees in two. I have come to cook
for a while, fold the clothes, closer

now to this ritual of discernment,
window, bird and book. They know
more birds than I could list in a year

of Sundays, recognize the whirring duet,
repeat visitors—two hummingbirds
who linger into dusk—even when names

of friends escape recall, their gray heads
bent to pane, as they wait, once
again, for the wings of grace.

Sorting My Father's Books

Hard enough to leave the gardens
where he planted four kinds of sweet corn,
trying to get them to fruit. Each year
the trees throw more shade
on his fertile plans. Hard to leave
the rhododendrons he bred, dusting
pollen on stamen with an eye dropper,
watching to see what golden peach
with frothy petals might earn my mother's
maiden name. Some surpass
the roofline, while dwarf varieties
fill wheelbarrows, spin the wind hot pink.

The cellos and trombones and tubas
he will store in the bathtub
of their Canterbury apartment, while
my mother claims in her next life,
she will marry a piccoloist.
Then there'd be room for fabric, aprons
for the church bazaar, Mason jars
of applesauce, pickles, beets, chutney,
jam. After all, eating must go on
whatever music finds a deaf ear.

The books have overwhelmed him.
Turning a few covers back, he insists
it's all a mistake, they should have hired
a gal to live in. My mother intercedes:
who would run the tractor, weed raspberries,
sprinkle copper on the mossy front steps?
Mold is growing on the grapefruit
near the shop, a red spider toying
with the rhubarb and they can no longer

[. . .]

climb the ladder to clean her kitchen
windows. Already my father runs
out of breath retrieving the paper.
The infirmities of the aged are legion,
he is fond of saying, quip from my grandfather,
who lived in this same house,
who also had to leave his books.

I begin the sort, stacks teetering
on coffee table, then floor and hearth,
finally on the continental divide
of the kitchen, where all comings
and goings take place, words
travel their circuitous routes,
generations hooked on the story
of the husky, dusky forest
I will always hear my father
reading, *Honey Bear* in his hands.

The Tempering

i

Evening, he laments the day's
small losses, robins in his voice,
trilliums in the damp woods.
Winter, he dispenses
antique remedies,
apothecary jars and quaint
urinals. The moon's an ember
in the sky, and the elms
are nearly blue with waiting.

ii

He comes for the crackle
and spit of pine, smells smoke
drifting toward the kitchen
window, open a crack.
On the wall: *Old doctors
never die. They just lose
their patience.* His legacy:
beakers of urine, of sacred
semen, tinged red as coals.

iii

High in the hills, the other side
of the river, *tools, all kinds.*
Among the saws and scythes
he brandishes a file, good one,
long and rough, no rust.
Held by his patient, one
he'd tried to save, and failed.

He pays for the tool,
cupping the widow's glad hand.

That night he lights a fire,
aged maple, and apple
stored in the tool shed.
It smolders till dawn.

 iv

A three-year-old
hefts a log onto the blaze,
kneels on the hearth
in pitchy jeans. Small hands
toughen on the bark
of fir, poke coals,
caving logs till they
shudder with sparks.
On the lake, mallards startle.

Hatchet in hand
children learn the art
of splitting kindling,
crisp wedges falling,
sweet sword fern at their feet.
Dust of triumph.

 v

The woods glow, twigs
buried in a mulch of ochre
needles. Soon we will feed
even his bones to flame.

Going Out in Style

Reckon I'll be gone in three months.
You never know. I'm trying
a social experiment. The ladies
come to supper all gussied up
well before the appointed hour,
lined up in their finery like orchids
on a lean branch. But the men,
they come drab as the boondocks
like they just got off their horse
out near Lexington or Castle Rock.
And we all know the farm's
long gone, no stallion's kicked
that field in twenty years.

What I'm fixing to do
is wear my bow tie down to dinner,
different one every night, see
if I can get a gentleman or two
to follow suit, come to dinner
like they are going out on the town,
like they really mean it. The ladies
deserve some civility. We only have
so long.

The Last Sleep

in my room
comes like an old cat

children's boots
line the porch

quilts no longer
hug my dreams

but theirs, and theirs
the pumpkins set out

under a far moon
of memories, lighting

the tips of dahlias
rains return

as deer
nibble new growth

on what I have
transplanted, miles away

their breath sweet
with fallen apples

Pleural Effusion

He cannot hold the long notes
on his euphonium, must catch another
quick breath, no rest in the score.

Tending his garden, he studies the four
elements: earth, air, fire, water,
transposes to another key:

sun, wind, rain, stone. He turns them,
rolling the words like pages of music:
leaf, bird, heart, song. Things come to him

as quarter notes, staff lines drawn out
on his yellow tablet. These days
he is cold, adds a jacket over flannel

shirt, gets his bearings, fingering
the valves: E flat, D, B, F, melodies rising
from the dust. A needle, under ribs,

pierces the inner chest wall.
He walks two liters lighter. Home,
declines the four corners of the bed,

fills the green watering can, measures
a quarter cup of cane sugar,
falling like sand. He stirs it as if

wielding a baton, carries the sweet brew
to the hummingbird feeder,
waiting: leaf, bird, heart, song.

Holding the Rain

Cupfuls in my hands, I am
rich in rain, rich in names
rivers that criss-cross
my town—Columbia, Cowlitz,
Coweeman, all streams
deep and swimming with rain,
running my name, birthed
with song, over the rocks

and downed logs,
over the snap of cork
rods, wallowing waders,
smelt nets, rain gurgling
along bridges, the high
train trestle we sneaked
across when nothing
was coming

My daddy loves a song,
pipes the euphonium
voluptuous horn some
call a baritone, mellow
notes holding the clouds, even
the rain, he plays
in the symphony, full
tux, but oh those dark bars,

barges floating on lines,
measure, measure, measure
he gets tired
of counting rests, the
strings have all
the melody of night,
nothing left to do but
unzip a cello from canvas

Hope playing
in his fingers, he settles
his thighs against the wide
bosom, rubs golden rosin,
drones long and slow
the bow quivers, starts to sing
even in rain he strokes the songs
loose, plucks the notes, raining

raining through the halls
of music, raining his river
down through the night,
the air still damp
when the theatre closes
its rained-out doors
He calls me Kibel, rainy
rendering of my given

name, calls by phone,
the old finger-ringer
we couldn't talk on
more than three minutes
'cause a patient might take
to calling in the rain,
needing something more
than the rain comin and comin

skipping down slurpy trails
on the rocky roads
in Cowlitz County, the rain
feeding the rows of corn
my daddy plants each
Decoration Day, packets of seeds
from Burpee's catalogue,
latest varieties of rain-

[. . .]

enduring grains, and the tart
apples in the orchard
all crooked in the spine
where the grafts took,
the gravensteins and the
granny smiths, the noble
delicious, and nobody minds
wet patches on jeans on boots,

on jackets, hell, we revel
in this holy water of old,
this way the heavens
have of tapping your shoulder
and saying, how ya doin,
sister? You been good?
Christmas night, my daddy
teaches the youngest cousins

how to hold a bow, how to blow
a mouthpiece all silver
all warm with his pursed lips,
he is raining words
in their tuned ears, he is
hitting perfect pitch
Ds and Es and Bs, he is
singing how to make

the music float in fifths, slur
in thirds, tonguing the trilled
tones, showing how to send
them belly hard
above the rain, sharps
and flats, salal and cedar,
how to carry the music out
in the dark to its natural

conclusion, he is
he is, he is stumbling
toward the chair, the sheets
of music fall, falling
on the floor, my cousins
call, calling his name,
his eyes fluttering his
ears his hands

They lift him, they lay him
they wheel him
out into the rain
cupfuls in his hands now,
how could he be not OK
in the rain, how could he
be, could he be
the rain, the rain, the rain

Going Up

When my father died, I kissed
his cheek, still warm, not yet
cooling to the undertaker's deft
touch, body bagged and draped
with red velvet, carried along
the short passageway from bedroom
to kitchen, then the remaining
distance to the whirring
elevator, final ride from top floor
down to first.
                    Going up, he always
asked if anyone wanted *six*, playfully.
There were only three floors at Canterbury.
Whatever was on the sixth, well,
something to wonder. No doubt
some thought of a billowy heaven,
clouds of archangels, or ferris wheels
rocking above the aches and pains
of this world.
                    Others jumped
to a confused mind, like the woman
living here, unable to find the right
room without calling each number
in turn and tapping the door
methodically, passing displays of china
in the hall—Lenox, Spode, Mikasa—
some relic of a happier time
when the closest thing to death
was the wild turkey stuffed and roasted
to perfection, sides still warm
as my father sharpened
the carving knife, let out its juice.

Breathing with Boulders

Skies undulate with the landscape
here—plains curving like blown glass
while tumbleweed skip the road,

bump along like gyroscopes
catching in the sage. Patches of snow
still cling to earth where rocks

shelter them from the afternoon
sun. Ahead, three horsemen, and dogs
guiding cattle down the gulch.

I slow, then slow again, keeping
pace with the land where I have come
to let the losses of the last year

roll out, their shadows lending
a cautious look back. Already
in the rear-view mirror the clouds

have turned steel blue. Now the cows
wend across my path, despite
running dogs barking commands.

I slow, and slow. One chocolate cow
meanders in front of the car, stops.
I nod. I wait, the revenant gap

between this one and a swaying
comrade growing. I allow
the space she has signaled, grace

[. . .]

seeping into my braked body
like a damp rain on the prairie.
I breathe with the boulders.

Finally, she resumes her journey,
deliberate as the wind on Highway 31.
Another follows. Another. I watch

the whole lumbering parade.
Such are the guides I am given,
timing exquisite as lichen

tracing patterns in the rock.

Cutting Limbs

Dead and gone. Some harbor green
core, tough to split. If my father could
see me now: pruning saw, nippers
alternating to trim the limbs, cut
coarse stock, leaves brittle brown.

In work boots, he would stomp the pile
to break what could be broken.
Those that wouldn't snap, he'd hit
over his knee, yank apart. More timid,
I try a thigh, jump when it works.

His stack went onto compost, or
bonfire fed by corn stalks, kiwi vines.
Intention: clear away haphazard limbs,
harbingers of death. Rake the final
stragglers into the fire, going full blast

to cover traces of what was, what grew,
what left, as all things leave, singly,
or in a grand havoc of heaps,
splintering mulch for memory, for what
will keep us in the long song ahead.

Morning Constitutional:

what my father would call this icy trek,
his daily discipline, an abiding brisk legacy.
The night snow has begun to melt, refreezing

on a gnarly pavement. Deer kick the crusted snow
like sand, belly up to the porch, recalling apples
from the summer roll-out. Walking sticks

invite some semblance of balance. My mother
bought a pair of grippers for my father's boots.
He never wore them, never wore gloves

while gardening either. He liked the feel of hands
harvesting spuds or carrots, running the tiller, pouring
oyster shells for chickens, oats for horses, pruning

wily Gravensteins. Protection from the elements,
a complex matter. After three pokes in the eye
with a cherry twig, he donned sunglasses on the ladder.

I tuck my chin so the stiff breeze can't nip my neck,
just cheeks, nose. Graceful limbs of Ponderosa,
white-shawled, nod encouragement. Wood smoke

flavors the air. A neighbor polishing his slick drive
redirects the snow blower's spout at each turn,
crafting precision rows like a corn farmer in another

season. Doves and quail hide from the noisy rumble.
I admire their patience, adrift in this prairie of snow,
gravel, tundra, pyramid caps on fence posts,

juniper berries deep in pillowed furrows.
On return, my father would pour hot black tea.
I simply change to dry socks, old feet

thanking me like a dog curled up on the couch.

Hill Haven

They aren't moles. I'm told nights are too cold for moles in the high desert. Then what -- gophers? Ground hogs? Prairie dogs? In the damp soil west of the Cascades, moles were plentiful as robins. My father got his supply of traps at yard sales for two bits, some farmer having given up the harvest ghost. Whenever hills popped up, he'd dig down a few inches and lay them in, warn us to stay clear. He didn't want an ankle enmeshed in the gears, a toddler's curious hand clamped to the earth. When he got one, he'd announce it supper-time, bury the sleek body in the apple orchard, or along the edge of the woods, where alder leaves made for soft mulch.

I never looked one in the eye. But I spotted plenty of mounds, out digging potatoes or tearing corn from the stalk, peeling broad squash leaves back for a golden bonanza. One year a new ordinance forbid trapping them, on account of cruelty to animals. My father kept up his solution despite the risk. He figured, more humane than shooting them, and no law against that. He was especially perturbed when they dug up the lawn, clipped short for picnics of a summer evening, cedar table re-varnished every five or six years to restore what wind and rain had roughed up. The trap wasn't an instant success. You had to wait for the critter to come up for air. It could take days, even weeks.

Here my hidden low-lifes stay quiet all winter, perhaps hibernating. But come spring, their handiwork pops up all over the yard. I scoop lush mounds into flowerpots for the pine seedlings that spring from ample cones. The soil is just right—combed and softened, free of roots, fine as biscuit dough. When I first started repurposing their primordial heaps, I feared I might slice one with the shovel, but it's never happened. They dig their tunneled dugouts well below the planted surface. And they won't cave in. When I tamp the excavated soil down, the lawn is flat as before the latest hill happened. In time the grass will spread across the brown moon, fill in with the help of whirling sprinkler.

We manage to co-exist. These creatures save their building frenzy for late at night when I'm already tuckered. When I open the door to a new day, I may find another hill to salvage for my tree farm, small but growing on the back deck. Sometimes I'm blessed with two or three, yards apart, a quick jaunt with the garden cart, sun on my neck. Life goes on as usual underground, my father's ashes on a tunneled slope. He is getting acquainted with new friends, inviting them to watch reruns of Perry Mason, where it all turns out okay in the end, his pipe smoke mingling with the damp and porous earth.

The Order of Things

    ~for Pam

Whenever my dad was asked what a friend
died of, he said, *he died of a Tuesday.*

Always a knuckle to the funny bone,
if anyone complained about too many
funerals: *it beats the alternative.*

I wonder if he might have changed
his mind by now, no longer needing

to remember his memory pills, or any
others my mother painstakingly
laid out. These he swallowed

without a sip, chugging them down
like a handful of peanuts. If they got stuck

he never let on, went about the evening
repast, first all his lettuce and radishes,
then all his corn, never varying

the course, alternating beef with zucchini
or carrots. When first married, my mother

thought there was something wrong with her
cooking, as he wouldn't taste one dish
before polishing off another. But no,

it was just his groomed sense of order,
growing up in Kansas where you'd better

eat while you could, not wait for seconds.
The only plentiful thing was the wind
rattling his sleeping porch, kicking up dust,

and then snow. He always ducked under
the covers, the air more or less filtered.

I wonder if he's met up yet with my friend's
dad, we poet daughters trekking to Iowa,
bringing images to pour from the hands,

like grain, to young doctors, steeped
in diagnostic tradition: constant queries

about what's gone wrong, tracing the phantom
in probing tests, thumping for reflexes,
turning an ear to the erratic pulse, the gurgling

lung, and listening, *listening* we urge them,
to what the patient has to say, whether

the affliction came on just last night
with the six o-clock news, or has been revving
now for months, sputtering in the cold

like the old Ford, building to a crescendo
cough with dreams that trouble them

more than the trajectory of breath.
Perhaps these two are telling tales,
bragging a bit, talking up the trout

they caught in their respective rivers,
one in New England where sunbathed

[. . .]

leaves are just beginning to fall, one
on the other coast, leaves floating
crimson before their crinkly drop. Maybe

they marvel at the reach of the cast,
or how holy the moon seems when it's

just you and a rowboat to worry about,
water dripping from the oars like words—
the girls would like that, they say—first a splash,

almost pleading, then a few silver pearls,
catching the light, dropping from the far

tip, coming home, coming home.

Messengers

My father caught them in his fist,
spinning as if to throw a curve ball, *zap*.
When he opened his hand, the fly
dropped to the floor. His gymnastics confused
their many eyes. He rarely missed.

This is where he shelled steaming crab,
newspaper spread on sandy floor,
his surgeon's hands taking respite
in the surf, casting for sunfish, ocean perch,
where he taught me to split logs,
one hand holding the splintering kindling
until just before the final hatchet slice.

I search the cabin for a swatter but none
materializes behind the fridge, the cupboard
with matches and flashlights. None
by the waders, the fishnet, the sweatshirts
stiff from salty wear. The kindling box,
out of paper. What can I roll?
A raffia beach mat in the corner of the bunk
room, too flimsy to hold a proper swat.

That high-strung buzz, incessant, now a dozen
zero in on the kitchen window, escape
barred by rusty screen. I flip pancakes,
dip dishes in suds. Two days I practice
tolerance, to no avail. They multiply
in my sleep. I am reduced to an avenging
fury. My yellow writing tablet threatens
near the sink, strikes in a frenzy of combat,
there, and there, *oops,* there. They hit
my speed bumps, resume their zoom, flee

[. . .]

to the picture window where I pursue,
waving my tirade of tiny complaints.

Days, before the cabin is completely
quiet. Dead flies dot the sills, pepper
the floor. A few, splat on the glass.

I don't know how my father did it.
He rose to orb-eyed challengers
the way he sucked in his gut
for a one-handed pushup.
At eighty he could still pull it off.
The flies have brought his antics
to the place where I write, fist opening
as words tumble out, their prolific
progeny stirring somewhere damp.

When I leave, I will pinch a morsel
of frosted donut, crumble it by the dish
drainer, where it will be taken
for an error, where it will convey,
finally, some small gratitude.

Elegy for My Father's Passing

The river knows its banks, cushions tender steps with sand, a few pebbles floating on minor laps, ripples on this scalloped table spread. What is served: memory, the chill of late afternoon, late coming. Here and there, a bit of bark with swirled eddies. A dragonfly dares a blade of grass, wakes you to the moment.

The river knows the bottoms of old boats, cradles them, receives their blue oars, the kayak's quick paddle, dripping the river back to itself like a dream playing over and over, color changing with the light: gray, tawny, amber, rose.

The river knows the mist that hovers, loose shawl about your shoulders, knows the time will come when the mist lifts above banked logs, silvered huckleberry leaves, the thicket of proud alders where once gushed flame. It will lift, and disappear, settling perhaps on the beaver, nosing the creek, or shrouding a mallard on the lake where licorice fern adorns the shallows.

The river trusts the spring surging through ancient rock, salmon berries riding the breeze on prickly branches, bright green algae pooling in still cul-de-sacs, feeding the slim fish that glide into dusk, or dawn, never sleeping.

The river knows what comes, comes again. Though you shiver in the cold and righteous night, spill a torrent of grief, though you holler in ravine-haunted hills, still a robin lights on a twig, cocks its head, apprehends all that is intended, jumps, and flies.

Acknowledgments

Grateful acknowledgment is made to the editors of the following, who published poems in this collection, sometimes in a different version.

The Blueroad Reader: Stardust and Fate: "Columbia"

Center for Poetry Newsletter (Michigan State University): "Going Out in Style"

Cirque: "The Tempering"; "Cutting Limbs"

Crosswinds Poetry Journal: "Reading Wind" (as "Minding the Elements")

Cumberland River Review: "Blessing"; "Going Up"

Elsewhere: A Journal of Place (Germany): "Hill Haven"

Evening Street Review: "Messengers"

Fireweed: "The Order of Things"

The Healing Muse: "Elegy for my Father's Passing" (as "Elegy for My Passing")

Interdisciplinary Studies in Literature and Environment: "Columbia"

JAMA (Journal of the American Medical Association): "Drug Thieves at the Doctor's Office"; "Pleural Effusion"

Nuclear Impact: Broken Atoms in Our Hands (Shabda Press anthology edited by Teresa Mei Chuc and Seven Dhar): "Baby Teeth"

Oregon Birds: "The Bird"

The Trumpeter: "Breathing with Boulders"

Twyckenham Notes: "Sorting My Father's Books"

Valparaiso Literary Review: "Morning Constitutional:"

A Walk with Nature: Poetic Encounters that Nourish the Soul (anthology edited by Michael Moats, Derrick Sebree, Virginia Belton, and Louis Hoffman, University Professors Press): "Breathing with Boulders"

Early Praise

Robin Meyers in a Beecher lecture at Yale in 2013 says, "Poets lead us to the edge of the river to drink without thinking they need to pick us up and throw us in." This is precisely what Carol Barrett does in *Reading Wind*. The subject of these compelling poems is her remarkable father, a country doctor, a knowledgeable naturalist, and an accomplished musician. It's impossible to give an adequate "taste" of the river water that Barrett's poetry offers to us, but in drinking the words of the collection, we feel as if we know her father and have always known him, yet grieve that we never actually met this unusual man face to face. There is no sappy sentimentality here, no maudlin eulogizing, but what there is in these amazing poems is an opportunity to drink into our souls the words of love for a life well lived.

—William Ellis, Ph.D., Professor of Literature
and Howard Payne University President (retired)

From the moment we enter Barrett's *Reading Wind* with a poem that elegizes downwinders, we are stunned into awareness of the beauty and fragility of the human and natural world, its joys, its potential loss and wreckage. In intimate lyric narratives, she invites us to live within the rich life and passing of her father—devoted physician, musician, and farmer who traded medical expertise for fresh-caught fish. His gooseberry harvest bubbled in her mother's pies; they bent together over bird books to identify cherished visitors. Even as his physical losses accrue, and they must leave their beloved home, his sense of humor leavens this book, as does blessing: grace reminds us to cherish the gatherings at table, in the garden, in the waiting room. *The river knows what comes / comes again*, she reminds us: these poems offer guides and grace notes for the joys and losses each of us has and will experience.

—Judith H. Montgomery, author of *Passion*
(Oregon Book Award for Poetry)

Reading Wind immerses readers in a delightful nexus of botany, biography, medicine, and memory. The poems reveal the world of a man whose passions for nature and music complement his professional pursuits, tending to the health of patients in rural Washington. Barrett's imagery is precise and loving, celebrating her father's life. In one poem we read of the *luminous microscope / still tracking the enemies / of men and rose leaves,* an image that springs from the context of a rural urology practice in which the doctor occasionally also studies roses from his garden. In others, we learn of his dedication to the local symphony, playing the euphonium and the cello, and his sense of humor, asking elevator riders *if anyone wanted six* in a building of only three floors. Ultimately, the collection turns to the author's grief after her father's death and the solace she finds in revisiting the land that he loved.

— Annemarie E. Hamlin, Ph.D., VP of Academic Affairs, Central Oregon Community College

A beautiful journey through a magical life of self and world, family and the family of life. The trill of a bird, the splash of an oar, the words falling from a pen—we hear the music of nature and of a doctor-musician joining in turn. We see doctor-farmer sharing the bounty with patients. These poems bring wonder, expanded consciousness, and also tears. Through his daughter's brilliant and loving poetry, we intuit in vivid and metaphoric ways, connections that were heretofore invisible. Although we lose this dear doctor-artist-medium at the end, we ourselves are changed—with new awareness, amazement, delight in each other, and in ourselves as part of this dynamic and ceaseless creation.

—Ruth Richards, MD, Ph.D., APA Fellow & Winner Lifetime Achievement Award (Div 10, Aesthetics, Creativity, and the Arts)

Carol Barrett grew up in southwestern Washington near the great natural forces of the Columbia River and the Cascade Mountains. This book, so true to the power and vitality of her home place, is also and perhaps foremost a love letter to a remarkable father. Doctor, farmer, musician, he could *read the wind* of literal weather or the weathers of illness in the patients he treated, who often paid him in produce of the land's bounty. Like the world as her father was uniquely able to read it, Barrett's poems are *pages of music*, passing on to us a profound medicine of *leaf, bird, heart, song*.

—Thomas R. Smith, author of *Medicine Year* (poems)
and *Poetry on the Side of Nature*

Congratulations to Dr. Carol Barrett for writing this lasting tribute to her late father. In this book of 20 poems, using vivid color and metaphors she paints a portrait of her father as a country doctor, musician, farmer, husband, and father. Using close observation skills and a penetrating voice, she describes his medical practice, love of family and friends, ability to play cellos, trombones, and tubas (and store them in the bathtub), *read the wind*, and harvest crops all surrounded by the flora and fauna of the West. These poems combine art and medicine and portray a country doctor's life and times. As such, it is an authentic and beautiful historical document of a phase of American medicine and also a loving tribute from an adoring daughter. As a juxtaposition of art and the history of medicine, it belongs in the curriculum of all humanities programs in medical and graduate schools, medical libraries, and hospitals.

—Paulette Mehta, MD, MPH,
Editor-in-Chief, *Medicine and Meaning*

Full of subtle linguistic texture and splashes of astonishing quotidian beauty, *Reading Wind* is both a tribute to the poet's late father and a tributary through places revisited in the aftermath of loss. Each poem in the collection is replete with natural images and reflections of the objects that make up a home as the speaker traverses the interior and exterior realms of heart, soul, touch, and color. Consider the *buds becoming / a quatrain of flowers* in "Blessing" or the *bristly berries / with limestone in the high shade / of persimmon.* In depictions of the outside world, the reader is invited to share in visually provocative elements of the living landscape; against that backdrop, the livingness that inhabits the inside settings is heightened, revitalized. This is a work of discernible unity and personal truth, a journey the reader may begin gladly and finish with a sense of renewal.

—Diane Allerdyce, Professor of Humanities and author of *Whatever It Is I Was Giving Up*

About the Author

Carol Barrett has taught Poetry and Healing courses for several universities, having earned doctorates in both Clinical Psychology and Creative Writing. She began writing poetry to support widows in counseling. Her book *Calling in the Bones* won the Snyder Prize from Ashland Poetry Press, following *Drawing Lessons* from Finishing Line Press. Carol also published creative nonfiction, *Pansies*, with Sonder Press, the first book in English about the Apostolic Lutheran community for outsiders.

Growing up, Carol played piano and clarinet; poetry became her music after several years as a choreographer and dancer. An NEA Fellow in Poetry, she has published in a wide range of venues, including *JAMA*, *The Women's Review of Books*, *Poetry International*, *Christian Century*, and *Poetry Northwest*. She also has published scholarship in psychology, women's studies, gerontology, education, and dance and art therapy. She recently began a program at Union Institute & University for students who are ABD, to enable completion of the Ph.D.

About The Poetry Box® Chapbook Prize

The Poetry Box Chapbook Prize is open to both established poets and emerging talent alike. The contest is open to poets residing in the United States and is open for submissions each year during the month of February. Find more information at ThePoetryBox.com.

2023 Winners

The Squannacook at Dawn by Richard Jordan

Inside Out by Kirsten Morgan

Reading Wind by Carol Barrett

2022 Winners

Tracking the Fox by Rosalie Sanara Petrouske

Elemental Things by Michael S. Glaser

Listening in the Dark by Suzy Harris

2021 Winners

Erasures of My Coming Out (Letter) by Mary Warren Foulk

Of the Forest by Linda Ferguson

Let's Hear It for the Horses by Tricia Knoll

2020 Winners

The Day of My First Driving Lesson by Tiel Aisha Ansari

My Mother Never Died Before by Marcia B. Loughran

Off Coldwater Canyon by C.W. Emerson

2019 Winners

Moroccan Holiday by Lauren Tivey

Hello, Darling by Christine Higgins

Falling into the River by Debbie Hall

2018 Winners

Shrinking Bones by Judy K. Mosher

November Quilt by Penelope Scambly Schott

14: Antología del Sonoran by Christopher Bogart

Fireweed by Gudrun Bortman

www.ingramcontent.com/pod-product-compliance
Lightning Source LLC
LaVergne TN
LVHW051112231224
799770LV00017B/582